ALSO BY MOYA ROI

POETRY

Out of the Ordinary (Salmon Poetry)

NOVELS

The Long Way Home (Attic Press)

A Wiser Girl (Wordsonthestreet)

SHORT STORIES

Other People (Wordsonthestreet)

Fire in My Head (Culture Matters)

Diverse Voices from Ireland and the World

Praise For Moya Roddy's Other Work

Out of the Ordinary

"*Stunning and memorable.*" Rita Ann Higgins

"*... a book of minute observations, of stolen glimpses and sudden seismic epiphanies.*" Jessica Traynor, *The North*

"*Each poem finds its careful focus, allowing us to remember our own lost moments and enter into dialogue with a poetic voice that is authentic and truth-filled.*"
Mary O'Donnell

"*The deceptive lucidity of Moya Roddy's poems of memory, family and often female experience in* Out of the Ordinary, *belies how very far from ordinary such directness and such perceptiveness are in poetry.*"
Leontia Flynn

"*... pared back and precise, quietly dramatic. Written with economy and intense focus—beautifully understated.*"
Martina Evans, *Irish Times*

A Wiser Girl

"*Normal People for a different generation ... full of verve, wit and compassion.*"
Mary Morrissey

"*a funny, fast-paced delight*" Nuala O'Connor

"*a total page-turner ... a love song to the journey of an individual told with a poet's eye and ear.*" Elaine Feeney

"*In these chilly, uncertain times, a blast of Italian sunshine, a sparkling glass of wine.*"
Ruth McKee *Irish Times*

Fire in My Head

"Roddy writes stark reality—her uncanny ear for dialogue places her like a kind of omniscient ventriloquist in these stories, lending a clear true voice to the truly voiceless."
Anne Cunningham *Sunday Independent*

Other People

"... the writing is so good ...the stories vivid, multi-layered, subtle ... with the sensitivity to language of a poet. Beautifully written."
Éilís Ní Dhuibhne

"... very much a literary writer, her breezy style borrows something from the best popular fiction writers; Wordsonthestreet have done short story fans a big service by publishing Moya Roddy..."
Kevin Higgins, *Galway Advertiser*

"Little time bombs!" Lelia Doolin

The Long Way Home

"... simply brilliant." Victoria White, *Irish Times*

"... a writer who attained 'a more complex and contradictory vulnerability' in her work."
Brendan Kennelly

The Day I Gave Neil Jordan a Lift

"...a genuinely comic story. This is beautifully judged and paced and as sad as it is funny."
Hugh Leonard, *Sunday Independent*

"Uproariously funny and poignantly sad—a short story par excellence."
Tim Goulding, artist

The Dark Art of Darning

Poems by
MOYA RODDY

salmonpoetry

Published in 2024 by
Salmon Poetry
Cliffs of Moher, County Clare, Ireland
Website: www.salmonpoetry.com
Email: info@salmonpoetry.com

Copyright © Moya Roddy, 2024

ISBN 978-1-915022-56-1

All rights reserved. No part of this publication may be reproduced or transmitted in any form or by any means, electronic or mechanical, including photography, recording, or any information storage or retrieval system, without permission in writing from the publisher. The book is sold subject to the condition that it shall not, by way of trade or otherwise, be lent, resold or otherwise circulated without the publisher's prior consent in any form of binding or cover other than that in which it is published and without a similar condition, including this condition, being imposed on the subsequent purchaser.

Cover & Title Page Image: *Young Woman with Ladder*—acrylic on paper by Moya Roddy
Cover Design & Typesetting: Siobhán Hutson
Author Photo: Jess Walsh

Printed in Ireland by Sprint Print

Salmon Poetry gratefully acknowledges the support of
The Arts Council / An Chomhairle Ealaíon

for Cassie and Dominic

Contents

The Dark Art of Darning	13
My Father the Biker	14
Breath Held	15
Old Bawn	16
Balancing the Books	17
Gumption	18
My Father's Daughter	19
Bad Boys	20
In Flight	21
The Promise of Snow	22
Gunk	23
Geisha	24
Headstrong	25
Fine Combing	26
Crab Apple Jelly	27
Out	28
A Taste for Words	29
TG Tips	30
Memoriam Card	31
Mammy, I hardly knew you	32
Make Believe	34
A Christmas Miracle	35
Magpies	36
Hindsight	37
A Sinking Feeling	38
Changeling	39

Waste Not Want Not	40
The Big Questions	41
Shifting Sands	42
Starting College	43
Mother and Daughter	44
Long Distance	45
The Girl at the Health Shop	46
Earth Bound	47
The Box	48
Life Lessons	49
After Words	50
Bliss	51
The Bookshop Cafe	52
The New Roof	53
Making Babies for Ireland	54
A City of Two Tales	56
Hell in Connaught	57
Snow in Connemara	58
First World Problems	59
The Paddies are Back	60
Forty Shades of Cream	61
Overnight	62
Pandemic Paradise	63
Scrabble	64
Birdsong/Warning	65
Free Lunch	66

Schrodinger's Hedgehog	67
Poppies	68
Swansong	69
What Lies Ahead	70
Saturday Mornings	71
Holidays	72
Visiting the Jopie Huisman Museum	73
Double Dutch	74
Reflections in a Courtyard in Leeuwarden	75
Birthdays	76
Understanding	77
Two Lighthouses	78
Dropped Stitches	79
Acknowledgements	81
About the Author	82

The Dark Art of Darning

I got all the practice I needed
on my father's heels; he usually
waited until nothing was left
but a gaping hole, a few stray wisps.
Fashioning a latticework of yarn
under – over – over – under –
looped either end to allow for give,
I wondered about the missing wool –
had it disappeared into thin air
particle by particle, or would I find
little heaps of fibres in his shoes
if I looked?

Darn these, he'd say, throwing down
a pile of socks and I'd see my
beautiful handiwork, my painstaking
craft undone – and – by dint of some dark art,
holes that were no longer his but *mine*.

My Father the Biker

Long before they were trendy
my father sported a leather jacket.
Despite the belt and oversized
pockets, it gave him a certain style.
And God, the smell! I'd nuzzle in,
inhale the heady aroma; imagine
him a daredevil biker, me his
old lady. Lean with the bike,
he'd roar, as we took a bend.
To spite him, I'd pull in the opposite
direction. Christ Almighty! D'ye
want us to have an accident!
Oh but I do Daddy. *I do.*

Breath Held

How I loved those early mornings,
mist rising, rushes cobwebbed, dew
washing my boots. And Daddy,
oh so cavalier, twill trouser tucked into
green wellies, sports jacket buttoned
tight, cap at a rakish angle; a point 22
cocked and at the ready.

Ssshh was the only word exchanged,
hissed if I accidentally spoke, trod on
a twig. Although all we were doing
was hunting foxes, crouched in a ditch
– breath held – we were, for a moment,
at one.

Old Bawn

Once when Mammy was in hospital,
Daddy took me and my brothers
for a picnic to a place called Old Bawn,
herding us across tussocky grass,
a small attaché case of egg sandwiches
in his hand. Plonking ourselves by a river,
we took off shoes, rolled up trousers,
paddled. What I remember is the humpy
ground, the embarrassing case, my father's
legs – pale – like creatures deprived of light.

Balancing the Books

My father did his accounts in a makeshift
office in the corner, entering figures in
a ledger, muttering and grumbling as he tried
to make them tally; **quiet** he'd shout if one
of us spoke; even though it was the living
room, we weren't supposed to breathe.

An insurance agent, he serviced the poorest
parts of Dublin, collecting miniscule
amounts towards premiums covering TV's,
cars, life policies. He died the year he retired –
leaving no insurance.

At his funeral, I bumped into a brother
and sister who knew him when
they were young: *Your Da was gas!*
Always laughing and joking. He'd play
chase, tickle us if he caught up. A real
saint: when Ma was short he'd sort it.
I could only stare. Who was this man?
Why had he never come to our house!

My Father's Daughter

Nothing was allowed disturb the ritual:
into the front room we'd traipse
(the one reserved for visitors)
Daddy's favourite home for Christmas.

He'd pour out two tots of brandy,
hand me a small panatela, hold
a second to his nose, to savour
the aroma. Women can't enjoy
cigars, he'd say, they haven't
got the patience, the implication
I was the exception. Inwardly,
I laughed (my mother needed
the patience of a saint); outwardly
smiled, complicit, hoarding these
backhanded compliments, never
giving an inch, never refusing
the brandy or cigars although both
made me sick: for better or worse
I was my father's daughter.

Gumption

Gumption was something my father admired,
his highest form of praise. Shushing us,
he'd turn up an item on the evening news,
read out a snippet from the paper –
Now *that* would take gumption!

It came back to me those dark February days
hearing of Ukrainian women and men placing
their bodies in the path of Russian tanks,
seeing footage of a man cycle past a line of them,
coat-tails flying – realising words don't always
measure up.

Bad Boys

Where did I learn to feel sorry for – even love –
the bad boys, the smiley boys, the sad boys,
boys who hung around corners, hands-in-pocket,
sex-in-their-eyes boys, cigarette dangling, winking
boys with too much oil in their slicked-back quiffs.
Boys grown to men with shabby coats, dandruff
on their shoulders, a reminder of hair plastered
across balding heads. Boys turned criminal,
monstrous. Cagney shouting –
Top of the world Ma!
                What made me want to be *their* Ma?
You're loved, I wanted to tell them, as I suffered
their shame, their need to be macho, not to lose
face. Did it start with the boy in the hand-me-down
gabardine, pants half-mast, who walked to school alone;
my brother choosing the wrong time to smile (*I'll wipe
that grin off your face!*). Or back, further – my father,
eyes pleading, asking, Who's Daddy's girl?
Who's Daddy's girl?

In Flight

There's no time to surf the net when
the call comes, just dash to the airport,
grab the first available seat –
and although the plane's travelling
hundreds of knots an hour my heart
outpaces it, each cell in my body
willing it on, assuring me you won't die
while I'm in flight, will wait – as you'd
always waited – until I get home.
I can still hear you from the top of the stairs:
What time do you call this, Missie!

Tumbling out of a taxi, I blunder through
revolving doors, down corridors, your image
large – to find you've shrunk, are tiny
in your hospital bed – asleep or in a coma
the nurse can't say: *Speak to him, they
sometimes hear.* Embarrassed, I whisper
Kojac in your ear. There's no response
but when I stoop to kiss your gravelly cheek,
the faintest smile appears. Have a cuppa,
she urges, plumping your pillow. I do as
I'm told; return to find you've slipped away.

On the flight home a thought circles: if
I'd caught a later flight or the taxi stalled,
would you have lived longer? Or like
the ratio of wingspan to fuselage,
a precise equation of length to breadth
that keeps a plane airborne, is each lifetime
so many breaths, so many breaths –
then no more.

The Promise of Snow

Not wanting to go in, I watch neighbours
scurry down the street, struggling
with shopping bags, their headscarves
pulled forward, collars raised
against a light fall of snow which melts
as soon as it hits the pavement,
while in the streetlamp's orbit
snowflakes blizzard – swirl and flurry –
evoking rooms festooned with paper chains,
lights tinselling a tree; a semblance of happiness
as the whole family – even my father –
tiptoe around the crib as though walking on ice.

Gunk

Gunk was a word
my mother used
for stuff she couldn't name,
whatever clogged the sink,
blocked the drain,
got onto people's shoes.
My father was more of a guff man,
could spot it a mile off –
was usually having none of it.
As children he cautioned us
not to teach our granny to suck eggs,
told us most things coming out of strangers'
mouths were all my eye and Catty Barry,
at best, a load of fanny.
Having an Auntie Fanny
who smoked a pipe –
for the toothache, she confided,
I guess I was prepared to swallow anything.

Geisha

My mother walks haltingly down
a boreen, hiding wildflowers behind
her back as though she's stolen them.
Bad health has exiled her to the countryside,
depriving her of her city garden, its lilies
and marigolds, Michaelmas daisies
and climbing roses. Her cherry tree.

An old photo shows a younger self
play-acting in a Japanese kimono
– the cherry tree in full bloom –
flirting as she peeps from behind
a painted fan, her free hand reaching
towards the future.

Headstrong

I was born on the South Circular Road
according to my mother; the nursing home
gone up in flames, along with all the records.
I warned them you were coming, she'd say,
getting into her stride, but the nurses were
adamant it was labour pains. Off they went
to early mass and out you popped,
bold as brass – a taste of things to come.

You were always headstrong, she'd fling
whenever we had a fight – wanting your
own way, never taking no for an answer.
Yet she connived in this: a certain pride
in her voice, a look in her eye as she said
the words; and I'd experience it again:
a violent surge, my skull bursting through.

Fine Combing

The fine comb had its own place
on the mantelpiece. Come over here
and let me have a look, my mother
used say if she caught me scratching,
parting my hair in smooth, rapid
movements, deft fingers examining
each strand, a shiver running through
my body. I'd pray she'd find nits,
all recollection of the smelly lotion,
the day of shame at school brushed aside.

I'm home, I'd yell and she'd fetch
the comb, pull me to her, drag it through
my hair over and over as I nestled against
soft breasts, her heart reverberating
in my ear, breath coming in warm waves.
I'm busy with your sister, she'd shoo
my siblings.

You missed here and here, I'd lie –
anything for a few extra moments.
That's enough, I've your daddy's tea
to get ready. At the sink, she'd turn rough,
allow soap in my eyes, dunk my head in
freezing water, shout at me to stay
still, stop wriggling! Even so, while
it lasted, she was mine.

Crab Apple Jelly

Mammy took a figarey the year
I turned twelve – the year everything
changed – ordering me and my brothers
out to pick crab apples. How we sneered
at the sorry-looking fruit: pock-marked,
disfigured, ugly as sin.

Once home, she dumped the lot in a pot.
Boiled, the mush was put into a white
muslin bag, dangled from a knob
on the dresser. For two days our kitchen
thrummed to a plop plop, liquid seeping
through gauze, drip-dripping into a basin.

Come winter, we heaped the pink jelly
on our bread, the gorgeous tawny blush
brightening those dark mornings.
See, I told my new self – face erupting,
breasts budding, the chafe of a pad
between my legs – beauty *will* out,
it's only skin deep.

Out

Where d'ye think reading will get you!
she'd yell, annoyed
at the sight of me – once again –
stretched on the couch, book in hand.
Go out and get some air!
                       Out I'd slink,
heart sinking. Couldn't she tell that characters
in novels were more real to me than all the girls
in the world playing hop-scotch, flinging balls
against walls, skipping between ropes without
ever getting tangled.

A Taste for Words

Mammy baked three different cakes
for Christmas, fruit, porter and a pale
Madeira. Once September set in
she'd start operations and for weeks
the kitchen overflowed with flour and eggs,
almond paste and icing sugar, there was
cinnamon and nutmeg, allspice, bottles of
tiny silver balls, counters high with bags
of raisins, sultanas, currants, candied peel,
even a see-through sachet of glacé cherries
guarded as though it was the crown jewels.
I nicked one once, popping it in my mouth
while she slaved beating sugar and marge
to a cream. It tasted sticky, insipid, unlike
the words rolling around my tongue –
glacé cherries, glacé cherries, *glacé cherries*.

TG Tips

My mother would have driven
a saint to distraction *Thanking God*
for everything. If He wasn't finding
her glasses, He was sending a bus
to ferry her home, a windy day to dry
the washing. He always knew where
she'd left her purse, made sure the fire
didn't smoke, above all gave her
a good night's rest. Letters to me were
dotted with TG this, TG that. Smugly,
I called them TG Tips after the tea.
It was years before I realised what
she'd been up to: connecting
the mundane to the miraculous,
the ephemeral to the sublime.

Memoriam Card

I come across it buried in a drawer –
the photo, one inch square, shows
a smiling face. I recall the original,
taken outside my door two weeks
before you died. A hint of cerise
from the sweater you'd bought three
days earlier lends colour to your cheeks
as you stand, arms outstretched,
palms upwards. Were you welcoming
death or was it a last embrace of all
you saw? There are things I'll never
know; the photo's cropped to size.

Mammy, I hardly knew you

You were everything
I never wanted to be
you were hanging out washing
sweeping floors, making beds
saggy breasts and varicose veins
growing fat then thin producing babies
you were everywhere
you were in the way

court shoes and slippers
double meanings and mixed messages
giver and withholder
go-between in-between
placater and protector
the patience of a saint
you were for making the best of it
finding the good in everything
keeping your voice down

ill health and doctor's orders
heart racing and palpitations
waiting rooms and hospital beds
getting sick and being sick
you wrote letters to your own mother saying
I don't think my daughter loves me

you were a keeper of lore
apples for moisture
salt in burnt saucepans
coal among lettuce leaves
egg whites to smooth wrinkles
brown paper vests soaked with
vick when winter colds raged

you baked apple pies and rhubarb crumbles
gur cake and lemon meringues
the best Christmas pudding I ever tasted
filled jars with blackberry jam and crab apple jelly
made two of everything
made things last

you read us stories with morals
Pinocchio Wizard of Oz
danced the Charleston
elastic stockings slipping
loved Nescafe and Fox's Glacier Mints
cleaned up shit and puke
wiped dirty noses
buried your youngest son

you delivered the Sacred Heart Messenger
with its lurid red cover
had a beautiful voice
loved flowers and gardening
looked young again in your grosgrain suit
and once when you unbuttoned your blouse
sat on the back step to sunbathe
you were sexual

brown Scapulars and novenas
rosary beads and memoriam cards
you went to Mass every day
trusted in God
not that it stopped us fighting
me attacking you deflecting
slow attrition

you loved your sons more than your daughters
had your own version of re-incarnation
hoping to come back as a snake or a flower.
I don't think I once thought of you as a person.
Mammy, I hardly knew you.

Make Believe

Granny made up a bed for me in the attic
the summer I was seven. Shrouded in black
from head to toe, lisle stockings wrinkling
over lace-up brogues, she looked like
a character in a nursery rhyme.

Downstairs, grandda eyed me over the rim
of his fob watch, a sleeping dog at his feet,
the fire in the grate hissing; unmarried Auntie
humming an air as she cleared the table,
a face on her as long as an ironing board.

Granny read me fairy tales – Hansel and Gretel,
Sleeping Beauty, Rapunzel. All I could think
of were the three storeys waiting to be climbed –
each stair further and further from the bustle,
at the top, a room with one eyeball of light.

Beneath the blankets, I'd listen out
for Auntie's footsteps, hear her hesitation
at the door, imagine manicured fingers
clasping the brassy knob. I wanted to cry –
Don't go! Don't go! Don't leave me here!

Mammy was red-eyed when I got home –
the hospital had run out of babies, she explained.
Later, as she tucked me in, I tried to tell her
about Granny's house, about the ogre-

Aren't you the great one for yarns,
she interrupted, turning off the light –
leaving me alone in the darkness.

A Christmas Miracle

Whisks came later. When I was young
a pair of forks was all you needed
to whip cream. A turkey spluttering
in the oven since Midnight Mass
 – the kitchen a furnace –
it was my job to stand in the back garden,
coatless, shivering, the bowl cradled like
a new-born baby, beating and beating.

It seemed impossible: the white puddle
sloshing and splashing, thin as milk.
All I could do was trust, believe, listen
with my body for that moment – the *turning* –
small peaks appearing as the first miracle
of Christmas Day took shape.

Magpies

One for sorrow, we'd chant,
skidding to a halt as we raced
to school, clutching our collars
to ward off bad luck, eyes
on sticks for a second bird,
ears alert for the ni-na ni-na
of an ambulance, the bark
of a dog, sounds that could
release us from the *geis*.

Even now, I search the skies,
scan rooftops, trees, listen for
a telltale rattle – despite knowing
nothing is as black and white
as I once imagined, that joy
carries sorrow on its wing.

Hindsight

As a kid I was obsessed with monsoons,
tornadoes, earthquakes; longed to live
in a country with extreme weather – unlike
Ireland with its soppy, temperate, winters,
half-baked, hardly *scorch you* summers.

Storms are so familiar now we give them
names, *Delia, Kelly, Oscar,* like long-lost
children rushing home to visit. Looking back,
I realise I didn't give two hoots about people.
What I craved was the might, the majesty of nature,
trees uprooted, buildings toppled, the earth
split open: a channel for my own destructive
forces, a child's will to power.

A Sinking Feeling

Nowadays it might be called a poor man's
Belfast – a ceramic sink with a wooden
draining board that oozed; home to hardbacks
– woodlice – that scuttled, died in puddles,
belly-up, tiny legs stiff.

I hated – feared – its sudsy depths, immersed
hands coming in contact with *things* that floated –
bacon rinds, gristle, gobs of lumpy porridge,
deeper still, knives lying in wait for bloated fingers.

Wanting rid of this symbol of poverty,
I bought a stainless steel unit for my parents
out of my first wages – only to see water pool
on its bright surface: discover an unalterable
tilt in the axis of our kitchen, the axis of my world.

Changeling

An early photo shows a chubby child –
mischievous smile cracking a cheeky face,
aged six you liked to belt out *Jailhouse Rock*
your pelvis putting Elvis in the shade.

As kids we played disaster games: plane
crashes, avalanches, space invasions. Down
you'd swoop – my invincible superhero –
to rescue me – a damsel in distress.

At thirteen, you discovered a vocation, left
home to join the Irish Christian Brothers.
A *changeling* took your place: a lank young man
who talked of sin, contrition, God's forgiveness;
warned me to change, mend my wicked ways.

Visiting you in hospital, aged nineteen – cancer
left you nothing but skin and bone – I cried so much
they barred me from the ward. Your dying broke
my heart but what was worse – the guilt I felt
not saving you from yourself.

Waste Not Want Not

You could drown in an eggcup
of the stuff, my granny was fond
of warning, not that we believed her.
Still, getting water from a well
was a tricky business: hunkering
down, bucket at an angle, a quick
steadying before a long sweeping
movement; pitched too low it would
graze the bottom, disturb sediment,
leaving an eternity to wait before
it cleared – faces slowly re-appearing
in the brightening dark.

II

Going for water was my brother's
job although I often tagged along,
helped carry the heavy bucket, hands
sliding, meeting, water sloshing.
When someone gave granny a statue
of a Dutch girl, all clogs and flyaway
cap, a pole on her shoulders, wooden
pails either end, I showed it to my brother.
Halfway home the branch broke, water
puddling at our feet. With a whoop,
we kicked off our sandals, jumped
and splashed. Nothing was wasted,
not even water.

The Big Questions

Propped up in your hospital bed,
the versions of you I carry in my head –
brother, writer, race-goer, friend,
crumble as I watch you struggle
to get comfortable.
The racing's on low:
a line of horses under starter's orders.
Racking my brains, the morning headlines,
for something to say –
(the big questions stare us in the face)
I'm saved by the tea-lady clattering in
rattling your elevenses onto the movable tray.
While you crinkle open a mini packet of custard creams,
I glance at the screen: two horses neck and neck.
A roar goes up, the race is over.
Is there anything better than a cup of tea and a biscuit?
you declare, a hint of your old smile.

Shifting Sands

The day you put the heart crossways in me,
racing full pelt across the beach, disappearing
behind rocks ... to emerge moments later
in your day-glo swimsuit, a quick wave
as you sprinted towards the sea. Dropping
everything, I ran, prepared to jump in
fully clothed – you'd never swum alone –
The triumphant grin you gave when I reached
the water's edge before vanishing like a fish,
leaving me to flounder, nothing
but sand beneath my feet.

Starting College

Once you've decided which clothes,
emptied out drawers into plastic sacks,
raided the hot press for my best linen,
we begin the task of squeezing
your eighteen years into a Ford Fiesta,
passing each other on the way in and out,
arms full or empty.

As the car reaches bursting you find
a cache of books in a cupboard,
a tattered teddy under the bed.
Too soon all that's left are scraps of paper,
dried up tubes of make-up,
an out-of-date bus timetable.
Spotting one of your old passport photos,
I slip it in my pocket.
For later.

Mother and Daughter

It's a mother's dilemma
trying to please –
I offered a summer's garden,
a landscape of golden wheat –
but she demanded pomegranates
although they were out of season.

Nothing I said could have stopped her.
I watched her go.
You worry these days
who's out there
which shadowy underworld figure
lies in wait.

And so she vanished; I went into decline,
withered,
the sap in my joints drying up,
my ability to thrive on hold.

When she returned – flowers
festooning her hair – the change
was obvious: blades of grass
sprung to attention, trees
unfurled pale nubs, even the sun
put in a milky appearance –
while beneath her feet
blood-red seeds bled.

Long Distance

My daughter the airline pilot, is how
you introduce her – a photo
on the mantelpiece. It shows a determined
young woman, strong bones, immaculate
uniform, poised in front of a Boeing 747.
Pressed, you confess you haven't seen her in years –
your lukewarm reaction to her choice
of career earning you the label *jealous old woman*
as she jetted out of your life.

What you don't say is how at the sound
of an airplane you want to drop whatever you're
doing, rush outside, wave; while at night,
waking to an overhead rumble, you lie
worrying about engine failure, bombs,
that she might not be getting enough sleep.

The Girl at the Health Shop

The new assistant at the health shop
nips out for a cigarette, hunkers
down on the steps behind the store,
inhaling deeply, eyes grazing the future.
You shouldn't be smoking, I tease,
sounding like my mother as she hides
her hands behind her back; realise
I could be her mother.

At the till we chat. My mother's
in Poland, she confides. I ask if
she misses her and she nods
as I hand over my Vitamin D.
For the first time I notice her
blemish-free skin, the diamond
sparkling in her nose. One moment,
she winks, reaching for a bottle:
this one does the same thing
but it's half the price.
Máthair, I tell her is Irish for mother,
Iníon means daughter.

Earth Bound

You were the talk of the town
with your star-struck eyes,
jet black hair –
dizzying about on stilettos,
head in the clouds,
décolleté before we knew the word.

You let me try on your silky dresses,
strut in five inch heels,
shared your dreams: a handsome man,
a big house, a girl like me
to dress in fancy clothes.

Years later, I heard you'd spent time
in *Pats*. Each neighbour had their own story:
The place was falling down;
the man a complete waster;
enough to drive anyone to drink.

Home on holidays, I passed you on the road –
moon-wan, your feet encased in flats.

The Box

The headless woman lived in a black
lacquer box. Unable to lie flat,
she crouched, bent double, sawdust

leaking from her body. Whenever
I took her out to play I'd make her
stand, walk, do splits. Dressed in

cerise pyjamas, trimmed with gold,
she looked Chinese but without a head
I never got to know her and although

I wondered what had happened I didn't ask.
Mammy left it to me among her things –
on opening the box I saw the woman

had vanished; in her place an angel:
Gloria in Excelsis Deo scrolled
between tiny ceramic hands.

Cradling it, I saw I'd lived my life
from the neck upwards.

Life Lesson

Observe, he orders, untwisting
the question mark, forging an armature
out of a wire clothes hanger.

Impaling a lump of wet clay on the uprights,
he strokes, smoothes, coerces, until
a female form emerges

neck torso breasts
mons veneris
the beginnings of thighs.

Holding his creation at arm's length,
he laughs, this is how I like my women.

After Words

When it came down to words she remembered
he never called her by her name, always *darling,
sweetheart, love, pet, poppet* one time.

And when things got rough the names changed –
cow, slut, whore, bitch; matching the bruises on
hidden parts of her body.

To her friends he was *the perfect gentleman,
the good father, the great husband,
the life and soul of the party* – *she* was lucky.

Their marriage vows were clear
until death do us part –
She left before it did.

Bliss

Not that long ago it was ducking into
shop doorways, behind sheds,
the back row of the cinema if the fella
had the dough; French kisses, love
bites, and (*oh teenage heaven!*) lurching
at the disco Friday night. If you fancied
someone, there was going steady,
anything above the waist; no one I knew
went *the whole way*, girls who did got called
rides, worse. Living together hadn't yet been
invented; your parents' spare room –
science fiction.

So much for the good old days, I muse,
waiting for you and your friend to
come down to breakfast. It's the first time
you've brought someone home and as the pair
of you squeeze in – sheepish – I nudge
your father's knee, wish I could say: relax,
your dad and I could tell you all about it.

The Bookshop Café

Regulars at the Bookshop Café
swap anecdotes over cups of coffee,
scones, warmed-up croissants,

regurgitating morsels of gossip,
when, out of the blue a small
dark thing swoops

windows are flung wide – efforts
made to shoo the pest out, a waitress
wrestling with french doors

as the intruder migrates to the bookshop –
is confronted by walls of poetry, prose, non-fiction,
a whole shelf on wildlife

choosing a volume the owner treats us
to photographs – rows of mouse-like beings
in damp caves dangling upside-down.

Unimpressed – stopping briefly
to skitter on half the Western Cannon –
the pipistrelle flies out the door.

Excitement over, customers return
to their now cold comforts. There's talk
of omens – of what no one's quite sure.

The New Roof

The new roof finally up, the old timbers
were used to make a bonfire, the whole village
gathered in a circle, drinking cups of tea,
cans of beer, somebody remarking that the wood
that was burning came from the far side –
a neighbour interrupted, swearing it came
from down beyond – a bit of an argument
flared, a young lad adding fuel, claiming
he knew, or his dad knew the person who'd
done the job, he was from – wrong again,
asserted the first speaker, my cousin was a friend
of his, he was related on his – the row rumbled on
as to who exactly it was, who knew who –
when someone else began reeling off the names
of everyone born under the old roof or married
out of it, those who'd emigrated, been carried out
in coffins, an elderly lady reminiscing that a few
generations back the eldest daughter had been
considered the best-looking woman in the parish
her husband putting in his spoke insisting that
was a different girl altogether because her brother
was the greatest footballer ever kicked a ball
but another oldwan called his bluff and a familiar-looking
man who hadn't opened his mouth said: would youse
listen to yourselves, anyone would think this was
a funeral! Look at that beautiful new roof – that'll keep
them dry a heap of years! Everyone raised a toast
– the fire spitting sparks like fireflies –
although underneath all the hurrahing and cheering
there was a kind of mourning as it slowly
dawned we were burning something
we could never replace.

Making Babies for Ireland

Where I lived women were at it hell
for leather. Two doors down was on
her tenth, Mrs in the swanky pebbledash
catching up. My mam with a measly
four lagged behind (dead ones didn't
count) the woman-across-the-street
who kept her kids in tea chests had half
a dozen, looked down her nose on anyone
with less. A slowcoach at the bottom
of the road was a source of much
resentment: some mumbling she was
nudge nudge not sleeping with her husband,
who did she think she was fooling with her
rhythm method. For years I thought women's
bodies were like balloons – blowing up
then bursting; when Brenda put me wise
I was gobsmacked. A bigger mystery
was where all the babies slept – houses
on our road had two bedrooms so it had
to be *ten in the bed and the little one said...*
What everyone did have was prams; wheeling
babies was big: girls loved it – chatting
above snotty-nosed snivellers about
growing up, making babies for Ireland
themselves. I wasn't as keen as Brenda –
I wanted to be an actress. Once, a rumour
spread a girl around the corner had jumped
the gun, was having one without getting
married. Mothers were up to ninety,
warning us to have nothing to do with her –
I was sure they'd have given her a medal.
Brenda swore when she had babies
she'd never let them cry, puke all over
the place; her husband would have to
stay home, learn to change nappies –

unheard of even for the likes of Mrs Kelly
who with thirteen was the clear winner
although Brenda's ma was always saying
have ye seen the veins on that one, she paid
a high price. Pure jealousy! Of course,
that was before I met the girl whose ma
had eighteen. She didn't know the eldest five,
they'd emigrated by the time she was born.
That was when I began to have me doubts,
were women really making babies for Ireland –
or was the country just exporting them?

A City of Two Tales

For some there's exhibitions, film clubs, book
launches, first nights and free-flowing wine;
there are complimentary tickets, oysters at the Oyster Festival,
vodka at the Arts Festival, mingling
at the Book Festival.

                For others it's the dole,
a tent by the river, a sleeping-bag in a doorway.
There are courthouses, Juvenile Detention, Direct Provision:
eat what's on your plate. There are no grant
applications to fill out; you are not being celebrated;
no one would dream of offering you a free pass
to anything.

Hell in Connaught

It feels like hell as you stumble
from a pub onto Shop Street,
pissed and stoned: one-way
arrows to the docks finally
making sense. In the middle
of the road, a half-dressed
youngwan evicted from *Heaven*,
Cinderella carrying her own
impossible shoes.

All across the city, mothers pace
their circle of Hell, wait for
sons or daughters to come home;
patrollers on the Claddagh keep
an eye on those eyeing the water.
All the same the craic's mighty
and if there's one less tomorrow
night, there'll be ten more the next.

Snow in Connemara

*"It's as easy to get a bag of cocaine as it is
to get a bag of sugar in rural Galway..."*

                THE IRISH TIMES

Trying to make sense of these words
I find myself drifting over the rocky
pools of Muiceanach idir dhá Sháile,
alongside the deep waters of the Inagh Valley,
past the sacred site of Máméan,
settling on a spot outside Oughterard,
a graveyard, a winter's night –
recalling a story in which a boy throws
gravel at a window, dies for want of love:
snow falling faintly, faintly falling.

Could lines of prose ever cut it
for those feeling the cold, catching
their death; or is that brightly-lit room
always the next fix away?
The lure of tinfoil: to live
a short distance from your body
if only for a while.

First World Problems

The electricity goes and I fumble around
the kitchen for matches. Locating a box,
I strike one after another in search
of candles, chance upon a couple of stubs
at the back of a drawer. Cursing myself
for not paying attention to warnings,
at least re-charging my mobile, I catch
myself on: all we're getting is the tail
end of a storm. On the far side of the world –
mudslides, floods, contaminated water;
people displaced, people dying; homes
reduced to matchsticks.

The Paddies are back

Christmas over, the 8.45 mail-boat
from Dun Laoghaire hoots as we lug
half-empty suitcases up the gangway;
doorstep sandwiches meant for later
opened as soon as we hit the upper deck.
We eat facing Ireland, watch the coastline
recede; and although gulls snatch
the crumbs tossed slipstream we'll find
our way home – again and again.

At midnight, we dock at Holyhead,
herded – eyes down – past customs,
security; unlucky ones stopped in their tracks.
Once through, we scatter like gunshot,
catch Pullmans bound for London Euston,
changing at Crewe for Glasgow Central,
Liverpool Lime Street, Manchester
Piccadilly, Birmingham New Street;
succumbing to sleep as wheels hiss –
the Paddies are back!
the Paddies are back!

Forty Shades of Cream

They were hardly in a wet weekend
before they painted the house a jaw-
dropping turquoise, not just windows
and doors but the house itself,
surrounding walls, a lean-to
at the gable. The locality saw red,
kicked up blue murder, who did
they think they were coming here
showing no respect for the countryside,
– blow-ins wouldn't you know –
and that place white for as long as anyone
could remember. And what was wrong
with white, if they didn't like it weren't
there forty shades of cream to choose from –
people throwing their eyes to heaven
whenever they had to pass the eyesore.
Before long there was something new
to complain about; besides the strangers
turned out to be just like them, sending
their kids to the local school, shopping
at the supermarket for bargains.

That seemed to be the end of it until
one day a neighbour's door was painted
a screaming magenta, an old outhouse
turned canary yellow and in less
than jigtime the entire townland
was a rainbow, know-alls at the pub
declaring it added a bit of colour,
hadn't they been saying that all along.

Overnight

Overnight the slight incline behind the house
became Máméan. Walking it, I could see
Croagh Patrick in the distance – a mound

of earth left by builders. A copse of trees
with a sprinkling of bluebells morphed into
Barna Woods, while a ruined outhouse straddling

the boundary wall was Aughnanure Castle,
the remnants of a famine village, depending
on my mood. Storms brought the Wild Atlantic

Way into the garden – barrels left out to catch
rainwater the nearest we got to Lough Corrib,
Nafooey; the day a frog leapt from one
I jumped for joy.

Pandemic Paradise

New visitors came – a pair of badgers that turned
the back lawn into a golf course, a vixen gambolling
with her young, a hare, ears alert, like

the one we watched on the runway the time
we went to Spain. Even a family of shrews showed up –
frolicking in the grass like wrinkled leaves.

Christmas brought our first graupel – frozen hail
that clung like magic to snowberry bushes.
With spring, blackbirds and wood pigeons sallied

back and forth – straw and twigs dangling
from their beaks as they made nests among
hazel, rowan, pines. May turned Mediterranean

and we lazed beneath our umbrella, marvelling
at peacocks with purple yellow eyes,
stain-glass admirals all the way from Africa,

speckled woods performing a mating ritual. Bees
buzzed loudly in the burgeoning vetch; roses,
cornflowers and marigolds came and went.

Great tits hurled themselves against windows
as if seeking a way in. We were almost happy
until we found ourselves eyeing the apple tree –
yearning for a way out.

Scrabble

It got us through the pandemic –
re-christened *squabble* as we found
ourselves arguing whether *gib* was spelt
with a g or j, *quoof* was even a word.
Eschewing a dictionary, never mind
an OED (abbreviations not allowed),
we had to learn to negotiate, accommodate,
take on trust. Not so much a game –
as life.

Birdsong/Warning

This year the choirs are in the hedgerows
singing singing singing
wanting us to stop
wanting us to listen.
They are singing our Hallelujah
They are singing our Requiem
They are singing their hearts out.

Free Lunch

It looked like a dry cone
fallen from one of the larches,
balanced precariously among

leaves of monbretia. On closer
inspection I realise it's a baby thrush,
a fledgling, feathers sodden, eyes

closed. I stand a moment, sorrowful.
When I look again the bird's eyes have
opened and I wonder if I should

place it out of sight of prey. Instead
I pray, calling on its mother, repeating
the words three times before returning

indoors. Later, I find the bird's gone –
flown away, rescued? Or have hawkish
eyes spotted a tasty morsel?

That kestrel we watch in awe
as it swoops, forgetting there's
no such thing as a free lunch.

Schrodinger's Hedgehog

After a couple of glasses we meander
in the garden, idle over whether
the hedgehog we chance upon
is alive or dead. There's a curious
cast to its eyes – open but unseeing.
It could be hibernating, I venture,
puzzling a moment over your perfume –
musk, a whiff of predator.

As we chatter about the possibly
lifeless creature, a raised eyebrow
or slightly furrowed brow the only sign
of unease, I wonder if there isn't more
to Schrodinger – wonder if being alive
and dead at the same time
isn't our default position.

Poppies

Poppies have made inroads,
seeding on disturbed soil,
making a stand against steel, glass,
concrete –
tossing outraged heads,
seeing red.

Epitaph I

We were busy having fun.

Epitaph II

We were busy.

Epitaph III

We were.

What Lies Ahead

For years a pair of long-eared owls
wintered in our garden –
once the cold set in they'd show up,
nest in one of the tall pines.
We came to recognise their tell-tale
shrieks – not the *toowit toowoo*
of fairytales, more the sound
of a creature in distress.

They seemed to tolerate us, circling
the garden at the edge of dusk,
light illuminating their feathers – until –
with a swerve of wing they'd vanish,
leaving us to the creeping dark.

Saturday Mornings

We sit in our favourite cafe –
on the table your Americano,
my one-shot, a plate of scones
glistening with butter, piles
of newspapers waiting to be
devoured. I go straight to
the Culture Section, you pick up
Sport; later we'll tussle over
who reads the Book Reviews first
– time expanding –
a small eternity.

Holidays

We talk incessantly on the plane
about the last visit, recalling
the things we'd fallen in love with,
you remembering this, me that –
the first sip of ice-cold vinho blanco,
a taverna we began to think of as *ours*,
how balmy the night air felt strolling
in shorts and t shirts, sandaled feet
resounding on cobbled streets, the way
lights from the ruins of an amphitheatre
threw everything into relief.

Visiting the Jopie Huisman Museum

A man of the people, my friend calls him
en route to the gallery, driving through
countryside flat as a canvas, windmills

tilted towards a vanished past, land I can't
see but know is there: a summer dyke
under water, held in memory until

winter recedes. She tells me about Hans
Brinker, the most famous Dutch boy who
never lived, never put his finger in a dyke.

Huisman, a humble rag and bone man before
turning to art, was inspired by the flotsam
of the poor – worn clothes, gnarled shoes,

misshapen hats. I'm drawn to a painting – a pair
of woolly drawers. The originals are on display
in a nearby case – knee length, baggy, faded

greyish-brown; patched one hundred and thirty-
three times according to the brochure, the thread
invisible until the woman's husband died.

After that, she stopped caring, used whatever
colours came to hand. Stories, like old bloomers,
hang on threads.

Double Dutch

After a morning at the Rijksmuseum, I visit friends
of friends, my head full of the richness of Vermeer,
Jan Steen's blowsy gatherings, am unprepared
for this Dutch interior, its cool minimalism,
walls and furniture eschewing colour,
monochrome prints, a glass table,
and – almost invisible – a small dog
asleep on a pale sofa.

Reflections in a Courtyard in Leeuwarden

Freesians often use their windowsills
as personal museums, filling them
with carefully chosen objects –
snapshots of a life.

Bunking off from a writer's seminar
we linger to admire one. I point out
a little shepherdess, wonder aloud
if it's Meissen. Catching sight of our
silhouettes in the glass, I notice your
eyes are on me not the figurine,
twist the ring on my third finger.

Clouds cloud the sun, our reflections
shadowed, under-exposed: something
that might have developed.

Birthdays

More! we cry, more! and more! and more!
but when it comes to birthdays we cry less.
Because more means less: of what we're not so sure,
and more or less we're happy as things are.
Yet life goes on and birthdays come and go –
Until one day when less means more
and every day's a blessing –
more or less.

Understanding

The prognosis is bad, you tell me,
a year at most. We sit in silence,
you with your thoughts, me recalling
a titbit that humans are the only species
who knowing they're going to die,
act as if they don't.
Want to talk about it?
Throwing back your head, you laugh,
offer a box of chocolates. I pick blindly;
watch – a bit surprised – as you read
each description, hum and haw before
finally choosing. Popping it into your mouth
you raise an eyebrow in my direction
and I understand – death isn't about dying.

Two lighthouses

Two lighthouses one red
one green one of them
a little further out
but so perfectly aligned
that from a certain point
only one is visible.
Returning along the beach
I stop at the same spot,
remind myself anything
can be skewed – moving
a little this way or that
can make all the difference.

Dropped Stitches

Noticing dropped stitches several rows
down, the beginnings of a hole, others
about to slip their moorings, I unravel
quickly. At the giveaway line, I ease
stitches onto the needle one by one,
ball what I've ripped. Holding the wrinkled
wool tight, I re-knit, repeat the same
pattern, aware of an absence – a presence.

Acknowledgements

I'd like to take this opportunity to thank the publishers of the following, in which some of these poems or versions of them, have previously appeared:

The Irish Times, Poetry Ireland Review, Stinging Fly, the North, Crannóg, Live Encounters, Windows 25 Years Anthology, Aids West Magazine, Local Attractions (Dedalus Press).

I'd also especially like to thank Jessie Lendennie and Siobhán Hutson at Salmon for publishing this collection and for their creative support; my partner Pete Mullineaux for support beyond the call of duty and my daughter Cassie who was invaluable in putting a shape on it. Thanks to Celeste Augé who read and commented on many of these poems and for great chats. Likewise, Annie and Ted Deppe for our ongoing poetry conversation. Thanks to Moya Cannon and Jessica Traynor for their kind and lovely words and my friends and fellow writers who are endlessly encouraging. Finally, my sister Ita who's been there for me over the years.

Originally from Dublin, MOYA RODDY lives in a small cottage on an acre of land at the edge of Connemara. Her garden is visited by lots of wildlife – badgers, foxes, hares, pheasants, shrews, kestrels and when it's cold enough, owls. *The Dark Art of Darning* is her second poetry collection. Her debut collection *Out of the Ordinary* (Salmon, 2018) was shortlisted for the Strong Shine Award. She also won a New Irish Writing Award, was highly commended at the Patrick Kavanagh Awards and shortlisted for the Hennessy Award. She has published two novels – *The Long Way Home* described in the *Irish Times* as "simply brilliant" and *A Wiser Girl* (Wordsonthestreet 2020). Her collection of short stories *Other People* (Wordsonthestreet) was nominated for the Frank O'Connor International Short Story Award and *Fire in my Head* (Culture Matters) was published in 2021. Moya attended the National College of Art before leaving Ireland for Italy where she painted for a couple of years. After moving to London she trained as a television director. *Que Sera Sera* which she wrote and directed won a Sony Award in 1984 and in 1985 the British Film Institute commissioned her first full-length feature film. Several of her screenplays have been optioned in the United States and she has worked for Channel 4, BBC, Scottish Television and RTE. A radio play *Dance Ballerina Dance* was shortlisted for the P.J. O'Connor Award and along with her partner Pete Mullineaux she co-wrote two plays for Galway Youth Theatre and the radio play *Butterfly Wings* for RTE. Returning to college she completed a Portfolio Course in Art at GTI in 2005; and was awarded an MA in Writing from NUIG in 2008. She has been facilitating Meditation at Brigit's Garden for the last twenty years – everyone welcome.

Photo: Jess Walsh

salmonpoetry
Cliffs of Moher, County Clare, Ireland

"Publishing the finest Irish and international literature."
Michael D. Higgins, President of Ireland